wave chasers 2

by jack nordgren

photos: jack nordgren–dirk sorrels & cam mammina headed out to surf in st joe mi. the noaa buoy showed waves of over 20 feet. the effects of hurricane sandy produced giant waves on lake michigan. these are two of my surf buddies. i call them when the surf is up. they surf more on lake michigan than anybody else i know. it doesn't matter how cold it is, it doesn't matter what conditions, if they can surf, they surf. these guys are two of my heroes!

ISBN-13: 9781477517611
ISBN-10: 1477517618

D1516910

dedication

this book is dedicated to my beautiful wife. she has put up with me for 42 years. i love her more than surfing-most of the time.

cover photo: mike killion -will wall -lake superior

4. lake michigan
5. will wall
6. brian mcdonald
7. ryan gerad
8. 3rd coast surf shop
9. brian lefeve
10. greatlakes surf
11. wetmitten shop
12 emilio moreno
13. mike miller
14. matt smolenski
15. eos surf shop
16. tommy shimetto
17. lester priday
18. blake meisinger
19. matt smolenski
20. roman vsycosil
21. johnny fox
22. lindsay simmons
23. will darling
24. bryon mason
25. sleeping bear shop
26. dennis sanchez
27. dairyland classic
28. lori westlake

29. beachnut shop
30 lake superior
31. erik wilkie
32-33.dana westbrook
34. justin burley
35-36. burton hathaway
37-38. will wall
39 keith hatcher
40-41. blake meisinger
42. a. brost & s.ronchetti
43. brent centracco
44. b. laddie
45. unidentified surfer
46. casualties shop
47. ryan patin
48. lake huron
49-51. james carrick
52. helene fillion
53-54. ronnie mix
55-56. josh gordon
57-58. matt walsh
59. jesse antler
60. bryon mason
61. endless surf shop
62. jack & jill surf shop

63. lake erie
64. kenny ashburn
65. larry cavero
66. mike roy
67. bill ulicki
68-69. steven bradon
70. kody kasper
71. mike sandusky
72. neal luoma
73. lake ontario
74. gavin fregona
75. rob dobias
76. shawn waitzer
77. elliot wollner
78. jeff gren
79. bradley van rooi
80. nadia baer
81. travis
82-83. larry cavero
84. atonio acuna
85. mike sandusky
86. josh davy
87. surf ontario shop
88. boards sports shop
89-90. about the author

mahalo nui loa (thankyou)

here's the photographers who contributed to this book. you left the waves to get the pics:
I couldn't have done this without your help

dave meisinger
peter matushek
mike killion
melanie lefeve
chris swart
tim haadsma
brian tanis
ginny fisher
nick vandersys
mike calabro
brian mcdonald
ella skrocki
marcie mason
joe horvath
bob tema
danny knowlan
heather landis
rusty malkenes
amber johnston
matt fritz
emily arnold
barry thompson

adam petengill
christine fillion
rob mcfadden
corey weichenthal
josh gordon
matt smolenski
george holmes
cole slutzky
mike sandusky
rich hunt
bradley vanrooi
gene neiminen
mrs luoma
gavin fregona
jeff hamilton
adam shepperdley
alastair macpherson
pulse imaging
john cavers
bruce reeve
rob santanello
ron harling

lake michigan

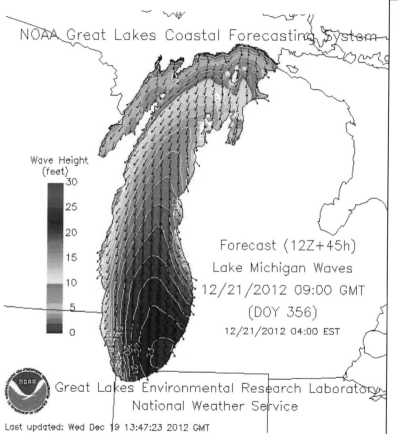

NOAA Great Lakes Coastal Forecasting System

Wave Height (feet)

30
25
20
15
10
5
0

Forecast (12Z+45h)
Lake Michigan Waves
12/21/2012 09:00 GMT
(DOY 356)
12/21/2012 04:00 EST

Great Lakes Environmental Research Laboratory
National Weather Service

Last updated: Wed Dec 19 13:47:23 2012 GMT

noaa wave map 12-21-12 (right) shows waves over 20 feet. lake michigan is 307 miles long, 118 miles wide with a maximum depth of 925 feet. there is 1660 miles of shoreline. the 3 things that create surfable waves on the great lakes are: the speed of the wind, the duration of the wind and distance over which the wind travels. the stronger the wind, the longer duration and the greater the distance, the bigger the waves. the best surfing is usually near a pier or breakwater. this cuts out the chop & allows the waves to have better shape for surfing. surfing on lake michigan is not limited to a place or side of the lake. depending on the conditions there can be surf in indiana, illinois, wisconsin or michigan. the men, women, boys and girls who surf come from all walks of life: from lawyers, university professors to construction workers. these surfers are my friends. unlike other places like california and hawaii there is a camaraderie between lake surfers. i hope this never changes. surf can come up at any time but fall is usually the best and if the lake doesn't ice up, we can surf all uear.

photo: dave meisinger-will wall surfing racine wi.. will started surfing in florida at age 11. later after the navy stationed him in san diego, his wife had their first child. they moved to wi. to be close to her family. "i'm still here. i've been blessed, and it feels good. i started out in milwaukee, surfed alot places fl., nc., nj, ca., mexico, hi., costa rica, australia and tazmania. hey it doesnt stop there, wi., mi., mn., and yes even indiana.." –will wall

photo: peter matushek (**www.matushekphotography.com**)–bryan mcdonald surfing the south end of lake michigan

photo: mike killion-ryan gerad-hangin out on the nose-new buffalo mi. 2007-ryan started surfing in 1998. one of his his favorite surfers is joel tutor. while ryan's surfing style has been influenced by many, his style most resembles joel tutor. his style is relaxed, fluid and he makes nose riding look easy but I can assure you it is not.

ryan gerad opened third coast surf shop in new buffalo, mi. in 2006, then 2011 he opened a second surf shop in st joe mi. they not only offer surf & sup lessons, they have summer surf camps for the kids. the shops carry boards, clothes, books, magazines along with wet suits. check out thirdcoastsurfshop.com and like on facebook or call 269-932-4575

photo: melanie lefeve-brian lefeve sup surfing silver beach st joe mi. brian and melanie drove from st claire shores mi. about a 3 hour drive. they were getting married the next day, i know because they asked me to do the ceremony. they opened a surf shop (23517 nine mack dr, suite b) in st claire shores mi. in 2012.

brian & melanie lefeve just opened great lakes surf shop in st claire shores mi.. besides having all the equipment you need for surfing, stand-up paddle boarding & kite surfing, melanie does yoga sup classes. brian does kite surfing lessons and they both do sup lessons. check em out at **www.greatlakessurf.com**, facebook or call 586-359-6951

check out wet mitten surf shops- grand haven, 301 n. harbor dr. 616-844-3388 & in-traverse city 101 n. park st. 231-929-3388 & on the web! www.wetmittensurfshop.com or http://facebook.com/wetmitten one more twitter: @wetmittensurf - opened in spring of 2011 by brothers john and ben mcneil. sup-surf-skate-kite-rentals-lessons

photo:go pro mounted on the front of surfboard-emilio moreno surfing the north side of grand haven pier, november 20 2011. he is originally from panama. he started surfing on an island called "isla grande" back in 1985. he moved to michigan in 1987 but did not start surfing the lakes until 2001. it actually was a surf shop owner in panama that told him about surfing lake michigan.

photo: chris swart — mike miller surfing "the elbow" in sheybogan wi. check out their surf shop, "revolution"
3347 kohler memorial drive ste 45, sheboygan, wi 53081 **920-451-0498**

photo: tim haadsma-matt smolenski team rider for wet mitten surf shops making a gnarly drop on lake michigan.

please check out mike miller (page 13) at eos outdoor & rev board shop, 3347 kohler memorial drive, sheybogan wi. 53081 phone 920-451-0498 also "like" them on facebook. they has everything you need to surf lake michigan, including surf lessons. not only do they carry surfboards, wet suits & sups, they have skateboards and even snow boards.

photo: go-pro-tommy shimetto surfing the south end of lake michigan. tommy and his wife courtney both surf. it isn't unusual for them to load up the surf gear and drive 3 hours from chicago to sheybogan wisconsin to chase waves.

photo: brian tanis-lester priday surfing wi. 2012. at 10 yrs old lester started surfing in austrialia. his dad wouldn't let him get a surfboard until he could swim a 1/2 mile. In 1979 he moved to the midwest. bringing his surfboard with him, after 2 yrs, he ran into another surfer and began surfing lake michigan. .

photo: ginny fisher–blake meisinger surfing "the elbow" in sheybogan wi. blake and his dad surf together alot. blake is still a teenager. he has been called by some a child (make that a teenage) surf prodigy.

photo: nick vandersys - matt smolenski surfing lake michigan. the outside sets were 12-15 feet. 6 were out, only matt went out for the big ones! matt is 30 years old and has been surfing the lakes most of his life. **www.surfgrandhaven.com**

photo: mike calabro-roman vsycosil surfing n.w. in.. i met roman about 2004 while surfing lake michigan (on vacation from hawaii). he gave me his business card. in 2007 my wife and i were making preparations to move to mi. we didn't know any realtors in mi.. I was praying when I came across roman's business card-he just happened to be a realtor.

photo: brian mcdonald-johnny fox surfing lake mich. he is 55 years old & still surfing. The Potawatomi tribe considers him an elder. he is an elder line-up too. surfing since he was 5. "i think we have a good, stoked crew here in fresh water, it's good to see people laugh and smile and share our surf"-johnny fox (check out his surf art on fb)

photo: ella skrocki-lindsay simmons at frankfort mi. she started in costa rica in 2008. she truly caught the bug. she says, "surfing is what allows me to maintain a positive state of mind and feel connected to my place in the world".

photo: ella skrocki-will darling (only 13 years old) going right at frankfort mi. he has been surfing since he was 6 yrs old

photo: marcie mason-bryon mason going right at seul choix pt. u.p. lake michigan.

__sleeping bear surf & kayak__ is northern michigan's full service freshwater surf shop! they are located in the heart of the sleeping bear dunes national lakeshore on the east coast of lake michigan. sharing their stoke by offering lessons, rentals and sales. surfboards, stand-up paddleboards, skimboards, longboard completes, sand bikes, touring kayaks, bodyboards, swimwear, wetsuits, lifestyle clothing and accessories and more. sleeping bear surf & kayak are all about encouraging free-ride play on the big water. they have been happily serving groms, families and people of all ages since 2004! located at 10228 w. front st, empire, mi. (231-326 wave) find them on face book or check out their website at http://www.sbsurfandkayak.com

this is a surfing family. mom (beryl skrocki) says about her children, "ella, the oldest was 8 years old and reiss was 6. they both jumped on a board and played in the waves that year along with us and then a year later they got their own boards. annabel started playing on a board when she was 5 in 2005."

photo: joe horvath-dennis sanchez surfing the elbow sheybogan wi. dennis is originally from hawaii but now living in southern ca. i met him at the dairyland classic (largest gathering of great lakes surfers in the world)

the "dairyland classic" is the largest gathering of lake surfers in the world. every year on labor day weekend in sheybogan wisconsin, great lakes surfers gather for fun, fellowship, contests, beer, and brats. they come from all over the united states. oh yeah, even from as far away as hawaii. there are team and individual contests and surf permitting even a surf contest. lee and larry williams started this event 24 years ago. these two brothers have close to 100 years of surfing the great lakes between the two of them.

photo: brian tanis-lori westlake going left. lori is a regular in st joe. she is one of the handful of girls i know that surf. many surfers put their surfboards away when it turns cold-not lori, she surfs all year. the only thing that stops her is the ice. oh btw way did i fail to mention she's a grandma? i call her the rell sunn of lake surfing.

beach nut surf shop has surfgear, skateboards, gourmet smoothies & souvenirs. they are located at 1100 main st, frankfort, michigan. you can find them on facebook or check out their web site **www.beachnutsurfboards.com** (231-941-5322 or off season 231-357-0690) open memorial-labor day.

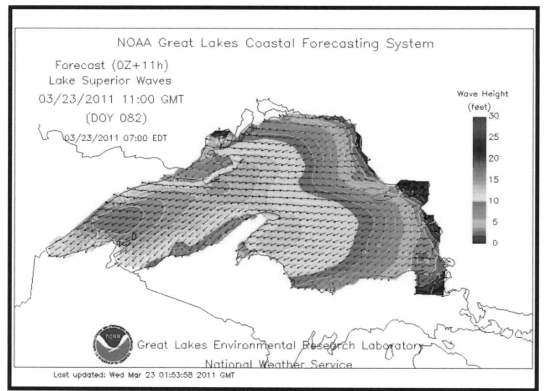

this noaa map from 11-23-12 shows 20 foot waves on lake superior (btw 30 footers have been recorded). lake superior is the largest of the five great lakes. it is bordered by ontario (canada), minnesota, wisconsin and michigan. it is the largest fresh water lake by surface area. it is 350 miles long & 160 miles wide approximately the size of the state of south carolina. lake superior is the deepest and the coldest of all the great lakes.

photo: bob tema-erik wilkie going backside on lake superior 12-21-12. erik moved here from ca. in 2008. he started surfing when he was 14. **check out on fb "AHBWI wood laminated paddles".** AHBWI is Ojibwe (chippewa) indian for 'paddle'...custom hand laminated, bent or straight. functional art from the northwoods of wisconsin.

photo: danny knowlan–dana westbrook going right on lake superior. i have been lake surfing since 1965 and this is one of the best lake surf shots i have ever seen.

photo danny knowland—dana westbrook sequence shot —same wave as previous page. man, I sure wish they would've called me and asked me to join them. it reminds me of a big day on the south shore of oahu.

photo: heather landis –justin burley surfing misery bay on lake superior. justin is a surf board shaper in grand rapids mi. check out his web site at **www.burleysurfboards.com**. it was so unusaully warm this day that one guy was even thinking of trunking it. superior is the coldest of the 5 great lakes.

photo: rusty malkenes–burton hathaway surfing lake superior with a rainbow in the background.

photo by bob tema-burton hathaway surfing on lake superior. lake superior is known for big clean ocean like waves. burton had a 8 hour drive to get here form racine wi. check out his blog at blog.nosaltsurf.com

photo: bob tema-will wall dropping in on a big one-lake superior. will lives in milawukee wi and drove 6-8 hours to get here. will grew up in southern ca and moved to wisconsin in 1995.

photo: rusty malkenes-will wall getting barreled on lake superior. rusty had to get wet to get this shot.

photo: bob tema-keith hatcher gets covered on lake superior. keith moved to midwest from northern ca.. he first heard of lake surfing after reading an article about surfing in sheybogan. he drove 5 hours to get there & met larry williams. in 1995 while driving around superior looking for surf spots, he met bob tema and the rest is as they say-history.

photo: rusty malkenes-blake meisinger getting tubed on lake superior.

photo: rusty malkenes-blake meisinger going off the lip on lake superior

screen grab from go pro surf video-alex brost & stefan ronchetti surfing on lake superior. alex and stefan are both shapers for idol surfboards. check out their website **www.idolsurf.com** or call 612-568-4365

photo: amber johnston (**www.thatgirlamber.com**) brent centracco going right on lake superior

photo: bob tema-b laddie lake superior

photo: bob tema – unidentified surfer on lake superior

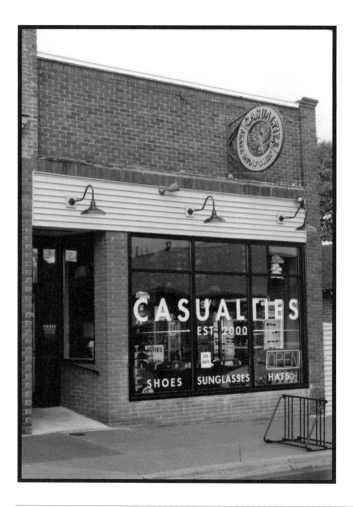

casualties is the u.p.'s (upper peninsula of michigan) leading retailer for all things skate, snow, surf, and sunglasses! opened in 2000 by brothers andy & matt jones, casualties has spent the last decade dialing in the product lines, so whether you need a new snowboard setup, fresh new shoes, or the latest sunglass fashions, they've got you covered.

located at 503 n. 3rd street in downtown marquette, michigan on (lake superior)

casualties is open 6 days a week. monday-saturday 10-6pm sunday-closed.

casualties can be reached here on ridewithcasualties.com, or by phone at (906) 226-8484. into facebook, youtube, or instagram? yep, they're on there too. visit their links tab for more info.

photo: bob tema-ryan patin going down the line on a huge bomb on lake superior

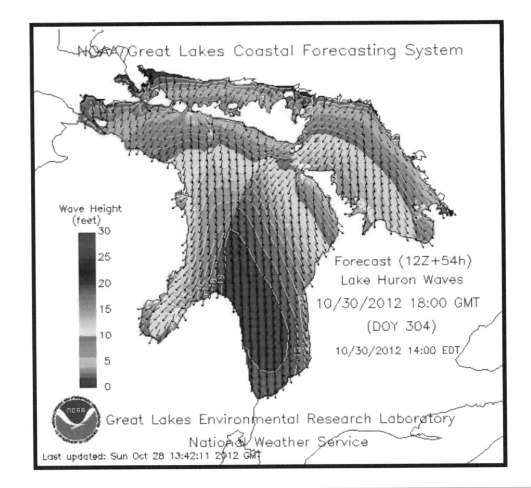

lake huron is the 2nd largest (by surface area) of the great lakes. it has 23,000 square miles. it is the 3rd largest by volume being surpassed by lake superior and lake michigan. it has 3,827 miles of shoreline. there are two surf shops in canada on lake huron.

photo: emily arnold-james carrick surfing lake huron. james says, "i met a generation of surfers, surfing sauble before me when i was 20year's old. i was an avid wind surfer, alway's wanted to surf. didn't even catch a wave my first time out but i was hooked—been almost 15 years—love every sec of it."

photo: barry thompson–james carrick surfing lake huron. james says, "were pretty lucky living on the escarpment having great surf on georgian bay and lake huron. we have some amazing spots–from pretty much every direction the wind can come from... check out his website www.greatlakesurfers.com

photo: adam pettengill-james carrick making a gnarly drop on lake huron

photo: christine filion–helene filion surfing huron. she started surfing about 6 yrs ago. she says, "i recently discovered all the other lake surfers near toronto. i got picked up and sponsored by "chick sticks" in sept and I'm really pushing to get more girls involved in lake surfing :) really hope for more girls to come out and learn".

photo: rob mcfadden-ronnie mix surfing lake huron-he started surfing by borrowing the lifeguard board at lakeside park to ride freighter waves. he moved to ca. in 1981 and then to hi. in 1993 and now resides in jacksonville florida..

photo-rob mcfadden-ronnie mix surfing lake huron. this is actually a sequence shot from the previous page

photo: go pro camera-josh gordon sup surfing lake huron

photo: corey weichenthal–josh gordon sup surfing lake huron. josh tried surfing in mexico 5 yrs ago and hasn't stopped since. he had no idea know you could surf on the great lakes. then he stumbled across some lake surf pics from sauble beach. the next day he ordered a board. after 2 years of surfing he switched to sup surfing.

photo: go pro—matt walsh going backside on huron. matt had a friend that told him that you could surf on the great lakes. matt told him that he was crazy. then 3 yrs ago matt tried surfing in califonia. he knew then that he couldn't live without it. he called & asked him where he could buy surf gear & has been surfing ever since.

photo: go pro cam—matt walsh surfing on lake huron

photo: josh gordon-jessie antler surfing with excellent conditions on lake huron

photo: matt smolenski-byron mason surfing lake huron. for board repairs-check out lakeshore surf on facebook. his shop is located at 15111 lakeshore dr, grand haven, mi. 49417 (616-834-5246)

endlesssurf shop on lake huron at **29 main st west, grand bend** ontario cananda. shop tel: 519-238-2813
rental shop tel: 519-238-8597 mobile tel: 519-476-2877 **www.endlesssurf.ca**

"beachin" 582 goderich st, port elgin, ont ca.
519-389-5790
"jack and jill's surf shop" on lake huron
214 main st, sauble beach, ontario canada
519-422-1440
www.jacknjills.net
live web cam at sauble beach, ontario, canada.
available from 6:00am to 9:30pm est during
kiteboarding/wake/beachin' season.
beachin

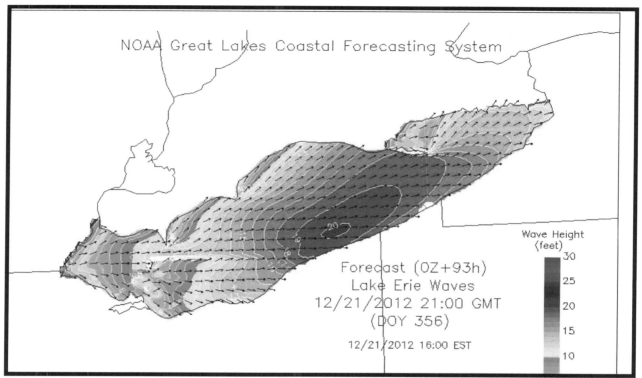

lake erie is the fourth largest <u>lake</u> (by surface area) of the five great lakes. it is the southernmost, shallowest, and smallest by volume. it is bounded by ontario on the north, ohio, pennsylvannia and new york to the south, and michigan to the west. the lake is named after the erie tribe of native americans who lived along its southern shore. even though erie is not one of the biggest of the great lakes, it still has the potential of producing some awesome surf. just check out these pics.

photo: george holmes-kenny ashburn surfing lake erie on magilla schaus' surfboard. magilla was one of the founding fathers of lake surfing. he was part of wlyewood surf club. after kenny moved to hawaii, magilla came for several visits. he was known and loved by many lake surfers. to say he was an inspiration would be an understatement.

photo: cole slutzky-larry cavero going right on lake erie

photo: george holmes(niagara on the lake surf club)-mike roy going right on lake erie

photo: george holmes (niagara on the lake surf club)–bill ulicki longboarding on lake erie

photo: mike sandusky-steven brandon surfing a huge wave on lake erie.

photo: mike sandusky-steven brandon on lake erie.

photo: rich hunt-kody kasper surfing on lake erie. kody moved here from ventura ca. after meeting kenny ashburn he says about him, "he brought me into the wyldewood surf club which has become my family".

photo: screen grab from bradley van rooi vids–mike sandusky going right on lake erie. go to youtube and do a search for bradley van rooi's lake surf vids.

right-photo: gene neiminen—neal luoma grabbing rail surfing lake erie 10-12-69. left photo: mrs luoma—neal took a vacation to hawaii 2007. neal is 62 years old and still surfs lake erie

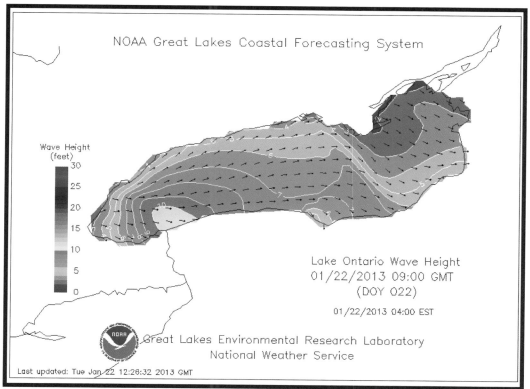

NOAA Great Lakes Coastal Forecasting System

Wave Height
(feet)
30
25
20
15
10
5
0

Lake Ontario Wave Height
01/22/2013 09:00 GMT
(DOY 022)

01/22/2013 04:00 EST

Great Lakes Environmental Research Laboratory
National Weather Service

Last updated: Tue Jan 22 12:26:32 2013 GMT

lake ontario is bounded on the north and southwest by the canadian province of ontario, and on the south by the american state of new york. ontario is canada's most populous province . in the wyandot (huron) language, ontario means "lake of shining waters". it is the last in the great lakes chain and serves as the outlet to the atlantic ocean via the st lawrence river. lake ontario is also the only one of the five great lakes not to share a coast with the state of michigan.

gavin fregona surfing lake ontario. gavin is 62 years old and is still surfing. recently, he had a hip replacement and was out of the water for 20 days. gavin says, "i started surfing in durban, south africa in the late 1950's. moved to canada in 1977 and just windsurfed until around 2005. saw a guy sitting on a surfboard in the lake catching nothing and figured I could do a lot better than that. had no idea that you could surf on a lake. so I built myself a surfboard out of an old windsurfing board and have been surfing here ever since. went to santa monica, california last year and surfed there every day. loved it."

photo: gavin fregona—rob dobias going for a cutback (almost perpendicular to wave) on lake ontario. rob is originally from north carolina. he now lives in toronto.

photo: gavin fregona—shaun waitzer cutbacks on lake ontario. shaun is originally from new zealand, where he started surfing at 9. after he moved to ontario, canda, he found surfntario.com—the rest is history.

photo: gavin fregona—elliot wollner sup surfing, lake ontario. he lives in toronto & makes surf trips to huron & erie. he says, " a six hour day-trip to huron and back is no big deal when the wave conditions are just right".

photo: gavin fregona–jeff gren at bluffer's park, lake ontario. jeff is 40 yers old he started surfing lake ontario when he was 16 years old in the beach area of toronto. back then very few people were surfing the lake .

photo: jeff hamilton (subsonic drone)-bradley van rooi going for a critical section in toronto on lake ontario. brad first got interested in surfing while on vacation in virgina beach. after watching for a while, he was hooked. he has been surfing on the great lakes for 25 years. this shot is from a cold day in january 2010. btw he made it!

photo-go-pro-nadia baer going right on her sup on lake ontario. in 2004 nadia began surfing in california then in 2006 she moved to toronto & quit surfing. in 2011 she discovered sup's & sup surfing on the great lakes— the rest is history.

photo: adam shepperdley-travis surfing lake ontario

photo: alastair macpherson (www.macphersonimages.com) has some of the best lake surf photos i've ever seen—larry cavero surfing lake ontario. also check out what larry is doing at surf dreams canada / online surf shop www.surfdreamscanada.ca (416)262-7532

photo: pulse imaging photograpy (www.pulseimagingphotography.com)–larry cavero making a radical cutback on lake ontario. pulse imaging began after they (mary lou naccarto & michele del duca) were asked to be photographers for the special olympics in london 2010. be sure to check out their website

photo: adam shepperdley-atonio acuna surfing lake ontario. antonio started surfing at age 11. he found out about lake surfing through an online forum but it wasn't until he hooked up with larry cavero that he really got into it. check out his whole story (http://glsurfadventures.blogspot.ca)

photo: john cavers (www.johncaversnature.com) mike sandusky surfing lake ontario. john was out looking for some wild life to photograph but all he found was surfers.

photo: bruce reeve–josh davy surfing on lake ontario. josh is a pastor (sounds familiar) who just started surfing a couple of years ago. "westmount ministries", in etobicoke, ontario canada. 416-244-7102.

surf ontario, 100 sunrise av, toronto ontario, canada www.surfontario.com +1 647-882-7873 surf, sup & skate-

store hours-wed - thu: 12:00 pm - 8:00 pm fri: 1:00 pm - 5:00 pm sat: 12:00 pm - 5:00 pm

BOARDSPORTS
Toronto & Blue Mountain

board sports store location

boardsports headquarters toronto

2010 yonge street
(5 blocks south of eglinton)
toronto, ontario m4s 1z9
canada

local phone: 416-485-9463
toll free: 1-800-665-9463
fax: 416-485-6065
email: customerservice@boardsports.ca

hours:
mon, tues: 10am – 8pm
wed, thurs & fri: 10am – 9pm
saturday: 9:30am – 6pm
sunday: 11am – 6pm

1st pic
charlie ammeson.
1967 st joe mi.
2nd pic ron
harling 1967
st joe
3-5th pic rob
santanello 2005-
2007 waikiki
bottom pic: matt
fritz 2008 lincoln
township lake
michigan

about the author–in 1965 jack nordgren started surfing lake michigan in bethany beach. In 1978, jack and his family moved to hawaii, but would still come home to surf the lake. in 2007 jack and his wife moved to michigan. he still and will always consider "ersula's" in st joe, michigan to be his home break.

jack nordgren lives in bridgman mi. he is married to his best friend maree for 42 years. he and his wife have 3 sons. they are all married and serving as pastors in athemn az., ventura ca. & honolulu hi.. they love to surf together whenever they can. jack gave God his surfboard and God sent him and his family to hawaii for 27 years, where they planted hope chapel in waikiki and of course, surfing was a big part of the ministry. in 2007 he and his wife moved to michigan, where they pastor south shore fellowship which meets on the beach (no kidding!). jack has three other publications, "a lake surfer's journey" www.createspace.com/3343542, "S.U.R.F. journal" www.createspace.com/3441835 & "wave chasers" (searching for surf on lake michigan) www.createspace.com/3825034 also at amazon.com

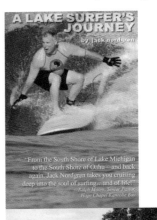

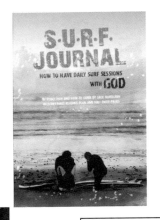

south shore fellowship meets at the weko beach café in bridgman mi. sundays 10 am (memorial day –labor day 9 am). for more info check out www.southshorefellowship.org

Made in the USA
Charleston, SC
01 May 2013